The
**Faith in
Action**
Series

Fighting for Freedom

The Story of Sam Sharpe,
Nat Turner and John Brown

Uzoamaka Agyare-Kumi

with Chris Hudson

Illustrated by Paul Bryn Davies

RMEP

RELIGIOUS AND MORAL EDUCATION PRESS

FIGHTING FOR FREEDOM

The Story of Sam Sharpe, Nat Turner and John Brown

It is the 1830s and the world is beginning to change with new marvels – steam power, electric light, machines that perform the work of hundreds of people. Inventions are making it possible to think and work and travel and communicate in a host of new ways. We can create, we can manufacture, and we can make money – there are so many possibilities!

But there are other questions too. Is it right to profit from the misfortunes of others? How should we treat those from other nations under our control? Do servants have the same rights as their masters? And the biggest question of them all – is it right to be able to control the life of another human being against their own will? In short – *is it right to have slaves?* Slavery has existed in the world for thousands of years, and the buying and selling of human life is still commonplace – but *should it continue?*

Opinions are divided. Many are speaking out against slavery, but it has its defenders too – especially those who have everything to lose from its abolition. Campaigns are being raised, laws are being passed. Old ways are being challenged – do we need to enslave people to run our farms and plantations? Is it really wrong to treat another man's life as your personal property? The debates continue. Tempers are being lost.

But slavery still persists in the Caribbean, Africa and in South and North America. Millions of people have owners, who declare it is just too profitable not to have to pay people for their work. In fact, in Europe it is unthinkable to consider a world without slaves, and those who make any protest should be treated

---

'It is a great and dangerous error to suppose that all people are equally entitled to liberty.'
(JOHN C. CALHOUN, AMERICAN POLITICIAN, 1840)

'Those who deny freedom to others deserve it not for themselves.'
(ABRAHAM LINCOLN, AMERICAN POLITICIAN – AND PRESIDENT, 1859)

'Those who say they're for freedom, and against arguing about it, are men who want rain without thunder and lightning!'
(FREDERICK DOUGLASS, AFRICAN-AMERICAN EX-SLAVE AND ANTI-SLAVERY CAMPAIGNER, 1857)

African-American: American whose ancestors came from Africa

harshly. They must not be allowed to get out of control, for what would happen if they did?

So there is a struggle of ideas – and sometimes, this turns into an armed struggle. But, when is it right to take up arms and fight for justice? How do you combat a violent system without becoming violent yourself, and making it worse?

This book will give you no easy answers, but it *will* show you how some people answered these questions, all at roughly the same point in history. Would *you* have done the same thing, or not, and *why?*

What Do You Think?

Important: In answering 'What Do You Think?' questions in this book, it is important that you not only state your opinion but also give as many reasons as possible for your opinion.

1. What do you think slave-owners were most afraid would happen if slaves did 'get out of control'?

2. In 1830, there were many inequalities in society. Think about ways in which people are not treated equally today. What groups of people are sometimes treated unfairly?

3. Like the world in the 1830s, our world is changing fast. What issues are making the headlines today? What are people arguing about in the media? Give some examples of conflicting views on one or more of these issues.

Fighting for Freedom

Fighting for Freedom

Where is Justice?

As Sam was brought up to the platform for his execution, there were shouts from the crowd.

'Hang him!' they spat. 'String him up!'

Sam simply stared back at them, then spoke loudly: 'I would rather *die* on those gallows, than *live for a minute more* in slavery'.

During this time of slavery in the Caribbean, Black people were regarded as inferior to Whites. They were not considered to be human beings in the full sense, but simply little more than beasts of burden, and only suitable for hard labour.

At this time, people were often referred to by the colour of their skin:

Black: dark-skinned people, usually African in origin

White: light-skinned people, usually European in origin

Creole: during slavery this term referred to an enslaved African born in the West Indies

---

As he waited to be executed in the Market Square, 'Daddy' Sharpe closed his eyes and thought back to the event that sparked this all off, the night of 27 December 1831. It had been his dream of a new beginning.

Sam the House Slave

Sam Sharpe was born in the year 1801, at Montego Bay, Jamaica. This was a time when slavery was common – it was legal to buy and own Black people as slaves, just as one would own a house. These people were originally Africans. They had been kidnapped during raids on their villages, then brought over to the Caribbean on ships as prisoners, to be sold on as slaves.

Sam himself was a Creole; his family were of mixed race, probably involving European planters and their African slaves. He was owned by a planter called Samuel Sharpe Esquire. A 'planter' was the term used for a person (usually a White man from England) who owned a plantation in the Caribbean. The primary crop grown in the West Indies at that time was sugar cane. Sugar had become a popular food additive in England, so the planters were able to use enslaved Africans to produce sugar on their vast acres of land. It was *very* profitable.

When Sam was born, he was named after his owner – which was the normal practice (i.e., 'Samuel Sharpe', but without the 'Esquire'). In those times, people who were enslaved were regarded as 'property'. They had no rights to anything at all, so their welfare and wellbeing were completely determined by their master. In fact, they were not even regarded as 'proper' human beings, but rather, as a 'lower' species. As a result, they were often beaten by the planters (in some cases to death), to ensure they were kept under control.

However, Samuel Sharpe Esquire treated his slaves with some care. He had different types of slaves on his plantation, both 'house' and 'field' slaves. The house slaves were normally of a lighter skin colour; many were the descendants of female slaves who had been raped by the (usually White) planters and overseers. These slaves were also called 'mulattoes' or 'coolies', and, owing to their lighter skin colour, were usually allowed more privileges than field slaves. They were also considered more appealing to serve in the plantation house.

Field slaves were generally enslaved Africans who had just arrived from Africa. They were usually of darker skin colour and were seen as more troublesome and unmanageable. As a result, they were treated much more harshly than the house slaves, and were not entitled to any privileges at all. They were also beaten regularly to deter them from running away.

There were other types of slaves too, with valuable skills and knowledge that were extremely useful to the planters, such as 'slave drivers' who kept the others in line, and ensured that there was order in the system. As a result of all these categories, resentment grew among the slaves, not just against their White owners, but also against each other. It created a hostile environment of mistrust and petty jealousies – but they all dreamed of the chance of becoming free people.

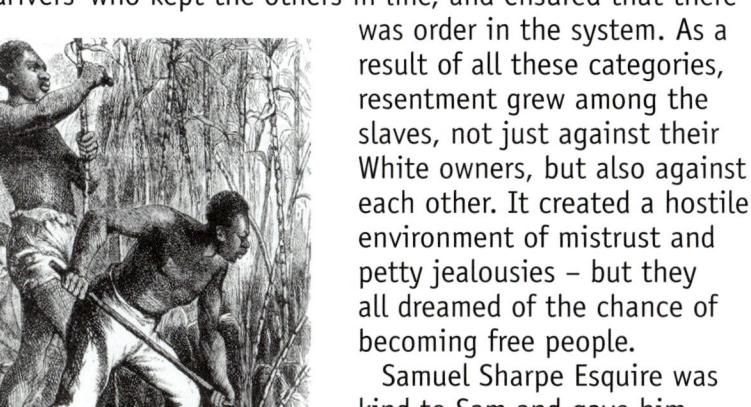

Samuel Sharpe Esquire was kind to Sam and gave him permission to work in the plantation house and not in the fields. Sam had been educated by his master and had learnt to read and write. Over the years, he was even allowed to read newspapers and other literature – something very unusual for that time and place. His good relationship with his master allowed him much more freedom than was normal for a slave.

Owing to their growing friendship, he became his master's 'right-hand man'. That meant that he was given certain tasks or chores that other slaves could not do, such as speaking on behalf of his master. One of Sam's responsibilities was to make sure that slaves who were hired out to other farms worked effectively, which meant that he visited a lot of plantations. He saw the harsh way the slaves were being treated in

Sam Sharpe

Field slaves cutting sugar cane

Fighting for Freedom

the fields – and realised that deep inside, he shared their pain and hurt. The beatings and arduous treatment given to them in the fields were very difficult to watch. Sam wondered how to help them. He wondered how he could make a difference.

> ### What Do You Think?
>
> 1. Planters treated some groups of slaves differently to others. How do you think each group felt about their owners, other slaves and their own situation? For example, did the privileged ones feel more free?
>
> 2. Why do you think the planters chose slaves to be slave drivers? Why did they group their slaves into 'types' with different tasks? Try to give more than one possible reason.
>
> 3. What does 'divide and rule' mean? Is this a good strategy for staying in charge or preventing change? What examples can you think of where this strategy is being used today?
>
> 4. Have you ever wanted to make a difference to an unfair situation? What might your options be if you saw someone being treated unfairly at school or at home? What risks would be involved?

Sam the Devout Christian

We do not know how Sam came to be a Christian, but we know that he was a devout believer and belonged to the Baptist Church. Some White missionaries in Jamaica (such as William Knibb) were fiercely against slavery. They preached from the pulpits to the White community about the injustices of the slave trade, saying it was a sin and evil in the sight of God, who created all people in his image to be free. In church, Sam began to think more deeply about how he could help stop this dreadful trade.

He began to read the Bible for himself, instead of just hearing certain bits read aloud to him. (In those days, slaves were not normally allowed to read or write, because it might give them dangerous ideas.) Sam's literacy helped him to go further in finding out more about God, and most important, that God loved him. He learnt many things from the Bible including the story of the Creation – and he understood very clearly that the Bible said all people are equal in the eyes of God.

Sam thought, 'If the Bible says this about the equality of all people and my master believes that, then I am equal to my master!' He continued to make progress in the Baptist Church community, becoming a Deacon and then one of the leading speakers in the Thomas Burchell Baptist Church. In time, he developed quite a following and became well known for his public speaking.

Deacon: a person who assists the minister in a Protestant church

His words came from the heart – he spoke with a passion that left his listeners feeling inspired.

Slaves were not given much time to themselves, but they were often allowed time to go to church. As a literate slave, Sam wondered how he could share his belief of God with his fellow slaves – and talk of the injustice of their situation. How could he share the Bible's good news of equality and justice? After much prayer, his life began to take a new direction.

Sam started travelling around St James and the neighbouring towns, visiting the churches and preaching about how slavery was unjust and against the will of God, and how important it was for Black people to realise that they were equal to White people. He told them that their masters had no right to hold them as slaves, no more than if Black people held Whites as slaves. The congregations listened and his words burned in their hearts. He spoke about how Bible passages had been used by some to deny Black people their identity as human beings. (The Bible story of 'The Curse of Ham' was one commonly used as a justification of slavery.) His words echoed what was in their hearts and minds – a sense of injustice and powerlessness, a lack of self-dignity and respect, and a denial of their self-worth and confidence.

But how could they become free, as Sam said? They had no power, no weapons, and nothing to fight with!

> *The Curse of Ham:* in the Bible, in Genesis 9:18–27, Noah cursed his son Ham – some people interpreted this as being their justification for enslaving Africans

'How can you talk to us about being free?' some of them asked. 'We are watched all the time. We are tortured for running away. Our children are sold if we do not conform. Our women and girls are being raped to bear more children to work on the plantations. We are told we are of no use. Sam, how can you tell us to be free?'

Then Sam explained his plan. There would be no violence, no guns, or any other weapons. They weren't needed, but his methods *would* bring the planters to their knees, if they were followed closely.

What Do You Think?

1. Slaves felt powerless. Have you ever felt powerless? If so, when and why?

2. How do people become powerful? What part does money play in making someone powerful?

Fighting for Freedom

Fighting for Freedom

Sam's Plan

In all his reading of newspapers and literature from England, Sam had discovered that White and Black abolitionists were protesting against slavery and the slave trade itself – and wanted it abolished in England and its colonies. A wide range of groups were behind this: many Churches were involved, particularly the Quaker movement. Some worked tirelessly in providing true accounts of how enslaved Africans were being treated. Freed slaves such as Olaudah Equiano published accounts of their suffering to reveal the evils and atrocities that the slave trade permitted and allowed. Campaigners such as William Wilberforce MP and Thomas Clarkson worked tirelessly to keep the slave trade on the House of Commons' agenda. Finally, an *Act for the Abolition of the Slave Trade* was passed in 1807. However, slavery itself was still allowed. (The Act only prevented the kidnap and transport of Africans across the Atlantic.)

Sam knew that many missionaries in Jamaica did not like the idea of slavery and were genuinely against it, but their influence was small. Many of the planters themselves were Christians – and regularly went to church. Yet they seemed to ignore the inhumane treatment of their slaves. It was the planters themselves who held considerable power in Jamaica and they had good contacts in England who would speak up on their behalf. The planters were *determined* that slavery would continue. Many of them depended heavily on using enslaved Africans to cultivate sugar on their vast plantations and they enjoyed their comfortable lifestyle. Despite the news from England, they *would* try to keep their slaves at all costs! (After all, weren't slaves their *personal property?*) Sam realised that the planters needed to be challenged on this and so he decided to organise all the slaves on the island in a joint protest. Quite simply, they would refuse to work.

Olaudah Equiano

abolitionist: a person who works to bring something to an end, e.g., the slave trade

What Do You Think?

1. (a) Why were slaves allowed to go to church but not generally taught to read and write?

(b) Sam was able to read and write. What differences did this make to his life?

2. How did Sam's Christian faith shape his attitudes towards slavery?

3. How did Sam's position in the Church allow him to influence other people and plan a protest? Was he right to use his position in this way? Give reasons.

'Daddy' Sharpe

Religious meetings were the only meetings allowed for slaves, so Sam used them to share his plan with as many people as possible. (He was now referred to as 'Daddy' Sharpe, although he was only 31 years old!)

'We all know that our planters love their sugar cane, don't we?' he explained at his first meeting. 'We also know that it will soon be Christmas, and we will be given a few days off to celebrate. And we know that they will want the sugar cane cut immediately after Christmas so it does not spoil. There, my brothers and sisters, is our opportunity. Let's refuse to do any work after Christmas – until they listen to us!' It would be the world's first sit-down strike.

Sam waited for a response from his audience, looking at the faces glumly staring back. There were mumblings and mutterings – but then one man said yes, this sounded like a good idea, and he would help. Then another did! More joined in. Yes, they *would* spread the news across the other estates! It was great news – and as he addressed more meetings, the number of people prepared to stop work with him after Christmas grew further.

However, a few were not happy with the idea of a *non-violent* protest. Instead, they wanted to fight and show their anger. They agreed with Sam that slavery was unjust and immoral, and only preserved a world where Blacks were seen as inferior and Whites as superior. However, they wanted justice served for all the atrocities they had endured and experienced – why *did* the protest have to be peaceful? This was a great chance to take some *revenge* and *everyone* would see it happen!

But Sam saw further than they did. He knew that the protest would lead nowhere if it became violent, and they would all end up being brutally punished. He also knew what the Bible teaches about methods of non-violence. Hadn't Jesus said, 'Those who live by the sword will die by it'? The planters had to see enslaved Africans as *fellow human beings first* and *that* would point the way towards making it possible for the two sides to talk to each other. They could then negotiate for themselves a better way of living together in harmony.

Fighting for Freedom

Sam chose some people to be group leaders to organise the protest on different plantations, and made them swear on the Bible that no violence would take place under their leadership. Yes, they would be rising up against their masters, but it would be in an atmosphere of dignity and control.

'Despite all we have been through, we can as a nation of enslaved people see beyond the pain that we have experienced', he said. 'We shall never forget, but we can learn to forgive.'

Everything was taking a clearer shape now. 'This protest will show the planters that we mean business,' Sam thought. He'd even planned his message to the planters:

'We want our freedom. We want to be paid for our work on the plantations. We want to have a better chance at life for ourselves and our children. We want to live well just like you live, as free people.'

He prayed that his dream would come true. His leaders were given final instructions and sent on their way – with a list of reasons as to why it all had to be kept peaceful. Off they went – and thousands of slaves made ready, all over the island. The date was set: 27 December 1831.

What Do You Think?

1. Sam wanted to protest but in a way that did not harm people. Do you agree with any of the reasons some of the slaves gave for using violence? Do you agree with Sam's reasons for not using violence? Do you think that non-violent protest is more effective in the long term? Think about any examples you know of where it has succeeded. Give reasons for your answers.

2. Sam said, 'We shall never forget, but we can learn to forgive.' Is it always wise to 'forgive and forget' (as the saying goes)? Is taking revenge ever right? Explain your opinions.

3. Why did Sam ask the slaves to 'swear on the Bible' that there would be no violence? When people in court 'swear' on the Bible or Qur'an to tell the truth, do you think it makes a difference to the evidence they give? Why?/Why not?

The Christmas Rebellion

However, some of Sam's group leaders had other ideas. They understood what he was trying to do, but this opportunity was too good to miss! A fire would *also* be lit on the refuse disposal shed in Kensington, North West Jamaica, the one owned by the Tulloch family. Everyone would see it and *that* would be the signal for a different kind of protest – a violent one.

As the flames were lit, some slaves began to set light to their own planters' houses – and armed themselves. The revolt had begun!

But the planters had plans too. Word had reached them of a possible rebellion and there had been whispers about Sam Sharpe and his meetings. The man was obviously a trouble maker, so he surely *had* to be the rebel leader as well! More of Sam's plans were discovered, before the date – which meant that the uprising came as no surprise to anyone – and professional British soldiers were ready to meet it with deadly force.

In fact, they were brutal. The soldiers showed no mercy. Unarmed slaves were massacred, and the bodies of the dead and dying lay where they had been shot. Some slaves were executed by hanging, without even a hint of legal process. Screams of terror and pain were heard throughout the island as the soldiers went about their grisly work from plantation to plantation.

Sam's non-violent protest had gone very wrong. With a few companions, he went into hiding, shocked at the way his plan had been misunderstood by everyone, both planters and slaves. Some of his people had suffered for too long – and only God could bring this terror, suffering and pain to an end, one day.

The revolt, with the soldiers' counter-attack, went on for eight days. Over 186 African slaves and 14 White planters died. After the fighting was over, a spirit of rage and blind hatred spread amongst the White planters: they wanted revenge for the death of their *own* people. Over 750 rebels were being held as prisoners, so the planters decided to make an example of them – and 138 were sentenced to death. Some were hanged, and some had their heads chopped off and displayed at various parts of the island, as a reminder of what would happen if other enslaved Africans tried to revolt again. The rest of the prisoners were tortured and punished so brutally that many more died as well.

Soon afterwards, Sam was captured and arrested, then imprisoned and put on trial before a jury of planters for being the ringleader of the revolt. No one was prepared to listen to his story or understand his reasons – the White community wanted to have a scapegoat: someone to blame for the deaths of the planters and the destruction of their property. As a result, Sam was sentenced to death. He was hanged at the Market Square in Montego Bay on 23 May 1832.

What Do You Think?

1. What more could Sam have done to prevent the violence? Was he being unrealistic, expecting the protest to be peaceful, or did he take a calculated risk? To what extent is there always a danger that things will become nasty when there's a confrontation?

2. How far do you think the planters' use of 'divide and rule' to control slaves contributed to the lack of unity which wrecked Sam's peaceful protest?

3. What sorts of choices do the authorities have when dealing with violent protest? What messages would different courses of action send to the protesters and the wider public? Is it fair that organisers of non-violent protests should be held responsible, and possibly tried and convicted, if the protest turns violent? Give reasons.

Sam the Unsung Hero

The Christmas rebellion became headline news in England. Some missionaries in Jamaica saw the brutalities committed on both sides as clear evidence of the need to abolish slavery and the slave trade. William Knibb, a member of the Baptist Missionary Society (BMS), was determined to preach against it, and do all in his power to 'slay the monster that was slavery'. He had known Sam Sharpe quite well and had encouraged him in his ministry. However, the BMS relied on the generosity and goodwill of the planters, and were unwilling to offend them over the issue. Before the rebellion, BMS leaders had warned William (along with Paul Burchell, another missionary) not to engage or interfere in civil or political affairs on the island. The pair obeyed this instruction right up until the death of Sam Sharpe, but even so they had made many enemies among the planters, who knew what they thought.

William had known about Sam's protest beforehand, and had tried to persuade his own church members away from carrying out any acts of violence. After his church building (like some others) was

William Knibb

burnt down during the rebellion, he was chosen to travel back to London to raise funds for rebuilding. This gave him his chance to tell people about the *real* causes of the revolt. He explained how Sam's plan for a peaceful protest had gone terribly wrong – and detailed the terrible acts of revenge that the planters had carried out on the slaves. At one of his speeches in London (to the Friends of Christian Missions in Exeter Hall on 15 August 1832), he said:

'I look upon the question of slavery only as one of religion and morality. All I ask is that my African brother may stand in the same family of man; that my African sister shall, while she clasps her tender infant to her breast, be allowed to call it her own; that they both shall be allowed to bow their knees in prayer to that God who has made of one blood all nations as one flesh.'

His speeches stirred a great passion in many people. How could such things be happening? His accounts of the atrocities caused a commotion – and many English people joined the campaign to make Parliament abolish slavery in all its colonies. They also organised boycotts of food and drink products that used goods, particularly sugar, imported from the Caribbean. Sales of sugar, cakes, tea and coffee all dropped! Signatures were collected for hundreds of petitions to Parliament, all designed to make the British Parliament listen to reason. Finally, they did. In 1823, the British Parliament passed the Amelioration Bill, which talked of abolishing slavery on a gradual basis to allow slaves the opportunity to live their lives as free people. Many abolitionists were furious at this – why do it *gradually?* This was just a delaying tactic! The campaign intensified. Then, on 28 August 1833, the Emancipation Bill was eventually passed by the British Parliament. Slavery was completely abolished in all British colonies by August 1838. It would now be illegal to own a slave for any reason.

Sam had dreamt of a world where Black people were no longer treated as slaves. It was finally beginning to come true.

Today, Sam 'Daddy' Sharpe is considered a national hero in Jamaica for his role in the events of 1831, which finally led to the abolition of slavery. His qualities of leadership, his organising ability, his presentation and communication skills, illustrate a man of extreme intelligence and vision. A statue was built in Market Square, Montego Bay, Jamaica to commemorate his prophetic vision and strategy for a world of peace and non-violence, and his face is also printed on the Jamaican 50 dollar bill. Market Square was later renamed Sam Sharpe Square in his honour. Sam's story is a focal part of Jamaica's history.

boycotts: protests about the actions of an organisation by refusing to buy their goods, or have anything to do with them

Sam Sharpe's story tells us that even during the time of slavery, amidst great horror and pain, it was possible to stay focused on the need to create an atmosphere of peace and love, and to stand up and speak out against wrong.

What Do You Think?

1. Why did the Baptist Missionary Society tell its missionaries not to get involved in political or civil affairs? What made William Knibb disobey these instructions?

2. Why do you think William Knibb's speeches in London were so effective in helping the campaign against slavery?

3. Why do you think Sam's story is still remembered in Jamaica? Do you agree that it should be told? Why?/Why not?

4. Whose life stories should be told in history lessons in primary schools? Choose three people and explain why you think their stories are important for young people today to hear.

Fighters for Justice

Across the world, there were many other uprisings against the injustices of slavery and the slave trade. It's a common belief that slaves never fought back, but this is not true – many did. Some resisted in a passive way, such as refusing to work or by going on hunger strike. Others were very active in their desire to be free – and a few led violent revolts. Some White people, disgusted at the evils of slavery, also felt compelled to take part in active resistance.

At the time, people who took up arms to fight agains slavery were considered by some to be rebels and traitors, and their histories were recorded with a great deal of negative bias. They had challenged the 'status quo' – the key beliefs of their rulers – and that made them dangerous. Their use of violence also made them hate-figures at a time when it was useful to blame somebody for social problems. Their families were stigmatised and isolated, and the real reasons for their revolts distorted. Nat Turner and John Brown were two such men.

Nat Turner (1800–1831)

Born a slave on 2 October 1800 in Virginia, North America, Nat Turner was raised by devout Christian parents, and learned to read and write at a very early age. His Christian beliefs convinced him that slavery was wrong and that God wanted him to challenge it. He was an intelligent man, but he also had disturbingly violent 'visions'. His fellow slaves called him a prophet. When a solar eclipse took place during February 1831, Nat took this to mean that God wanted him to create an armed slave rebellion on 4 July, Independence Day. However, Nat was taken ill – and the revolt was postponed. On 13 August, he saw another 'sign' in the sun, and explained that this was God's signal to continue the rebellion.

It started in Southampton County, Virginia, on the night of Sunday 21 August. Nat's small group were already armed, but they stole more guns, swords and machetes as they went from house to house, freeing slaves and killing any White people who lived there – including the women and children. Other slaves joined Nat's group, which grew to about 40 in number, but they were finally confronted and attacked by an armed militia of local White people. (Some Black slaves also resisted the revolt, believing it to be wrong, and wanting to help save lives.) The rebel band were scattered and quickly captured – after only two days.

Nat escaped, but he was eventually discovered hiding in a canal. He was arrested and, on 5 November, tried and sentenced to death. However, after the sentence was passed, he had the opportunity to talk to Thomas R. Gray, a journalist. Over three days, Nat told both his story and the reasons for his fight against slavery and the maltreatment of slaves. It was later published as *The Confessions of Nat Turner* and sold many copies, having to be re-published several times to meet customer demand. His execution took place on 11 November 1831. His body was mutilated, cut into several pieces, and the body parts were distributed to various White planter families for souvenirs, as a warning to other rebel slaves.

These events caused a great stir throughout Virginia and the Southern States – and a thirst for revenge. Other slave suspects, 55 in total, were also executed, and hundreds of innocent slaves were tortured and murdered by angry White vigilante mobs. A lasting fear of slave revolts had set in. Would others be following Nat's example? Was slavery itself to blame? Was more bloodshed inevitable? Some Virginian politicians actually called for slavery to be abolished in their state, but most White people were too scared to consider it – so instead, they passed even tougher laws. Freed slaves were forced to become slaves again and abolitionists were legally prevented from speaking out. Discussing slavery became illegal!

vigilante: a person who 'takes the law into their own hands' and punishes others for wrong doings

Nat Turner's rebellion raised important questions about whether it was right to keep slaves – but it raised fears and hardened attitudes in the South against abolition, making the lives of many slaves much more difficult. However, Nat's vision and thirst for freedom, and the price he paid for it, are still recognised by African-Americans today.

What Do You Think?

1. How do you think the slaves justified killing the planters and their families? What circumstances can you think of when it could be right to kill another person? Explain why.

2. Nat sincerely believed his visions came from God and that, in leading the revolt, he was acting according to God's will. Some Christians or other religious believers might have disagreed with Nat about this. What do you think they might have said?

Fighting for Freedom

15

John Brown (1800–1859)

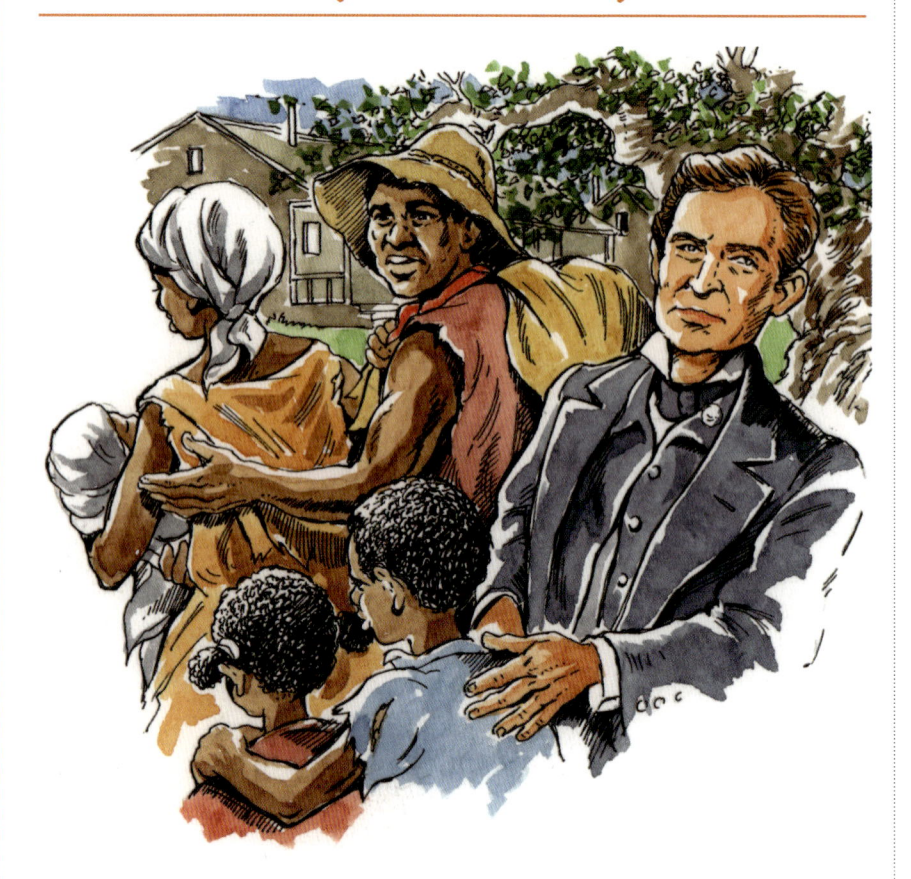

Slavery was violently resisted by White people too – this is the story of one of the most famous to do so.

John Brown was born to a White family in Torrington, Connecticut, on 9 May 1800. He was brought up by his parents to study the Bible and to hate slavery. He married and had many children, making his living initially as a self-employed 'tanner' – making leather from animal hides. This was the first of many efforts at running a business to support his large and growing family.

During these early years, John was increasingly angry at the way Black people were treated as slaves. He personally witnessed several acts of cruelty being committed against them and was horrified that such acts were legal. As a parent, he instilled in his own children the need to respect the dignity of all God's people, but this wasn't enough. Slavery outraged him! Wasn't there something more he could do?

John tried to establish himself as a builder, a landowner and then as a sheep farmer, but none of these enterprises quite worked out: his thoughts were increasingly gripped by a powerful desire to bring about real justice for Black people and make a stand against slavery. He spent more time with them, asking questions and hearing their concerns – and lived for two years with a community of freed African slaves in North Elba, New York. By 1855, he was a conductor on the 'Underground Railroad', and a local organiser of a group protecting fugitive slaves and free Black people.

In August 1855, John travelled to Kansas with five of his sons to help the state create a safe haven for anti-slavery settlers. There was so much hostility to this work that in 1856 some pro-slavery activists decided to hit back. The free-state community of Lawrence was attacked by armed men who burnt the whole town to the ground – then massacred all the inhabitants.

This was a turning point for John. *Someone* had to

The Underground Railroad was a secret network of 'safe houses' and transport routes that helped runaway slaves escape North to places where slavery was illegal, such as Canada. The routes were serviced by Black and White volunteers who provided shelter, food and clothes for the fugitives. Famous volunteers included William Still, and ex-slaves such as Frederick Douglass and Harriet Tubman (1820–1897).

Harriet Tubman was born to enslaved African parents living in Maryland and hired out as a worker by the age of five. At the age of 15 (already known as an unwilling servant), she was beaten for helping a runaway slave: the blow left her with permanent brain injuries causing sudden fainting spells. In 1849, she used the Underground Railroad to escape North, but returned in later years as one of its most famous 'conductors' to rescue both her own family and many other slaves seeking freedom. In all, she made 19 trips back South to rescue over 300 people. A $40 000 reward was put on her head, but she was never caught – and later served as a spy for the Union Army during the Civil War. She always expressed confidence that God would aid her efforts, and threatened to shoot any of her charges who wanted to turn back. According to John Brown, she was one of the 'bravest persons on this continent'.

North: in the American Civil War the Northern States, the Unionists, had become industrialised and used immigrant labour rather than slaves

South: in the American Civil War the Southern States, the Confederates, were dependent on slaves for their economy

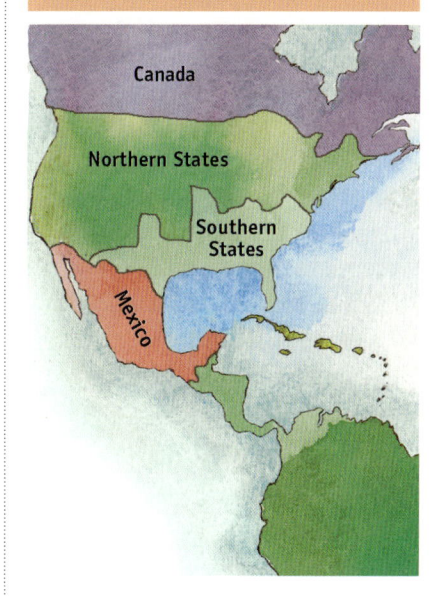

fight back against this brutality! He organised a militia unit of armed volunteers from his own Osawatomie River colony and led them out on a mission of revenge. On the night of 23 May 1856, John and six followers (four of whom were his sons) attacked the homes of several pro-slavery activists along Pottawatomie Creek. His victims were dragged out of their homes and executed with long-edged swords.

News of their deaths spread across the state like wildfire. 'Old Brown Osawatomie' (John's nickname) became a hate-figure across the Southern slave states. He now wanted to go further and free more slaves, so he travelled back to Ohio to organise further revolts. There was no going back: his rich supporters in New England were only too ready to finance his war, so he went on to raid plantations in Missouri. In the summer of 1859, John changed his tactics. His new plan was to provide guns and ammunition for thousands of Black slaves to defend themselves and form a freedom army – by raiding a large government armoury and arsenal at Harpers Ferry in Western Virginia. His small attack force even included some freed slaves – this would be a turning point in the history of North America!

Fighting for Freedom

Fighting for Freedom

One of John's favourite Bible quotes was:

'Without the shedding of blood there is no forgiveness of sins.'
(Hebrews 9:22)

Most Christians understand this to refer to Jesus shedding his blood when he was crucified. They believe that this means that God will forgive the wrong things they do. John understood this Bible teaching differently – he thought that slavery was wrong; it was a sin. So he reasoned that to remove the sin of slavery, blood had to be shed, and he planned his raid regardless of the risk of bloodshed and death. But the raid was badly planned. John's group made their attack on 16 October 1859. They were quickly surrounded and had to retreat inside the local fire-engine house. There was a short armed siege of the building; John was finally wounded and captured with seven of his men. Another ten died in the fighting.

John was arrested, taken to Charlestown and put on trial. In court, he made it clear that he thought the injustices committed against Black people were unacceptable to God, and that slavery was evil – it was every man's responsibility to ensure that all men were considered equal! He was found guilty of treason and hanged on 2 December, amidst great public rejoicing. The hated enemy had been struck down!

However, his sacrifice became a rallying point for the abolition movement. On the day of his execution, bells were tolled in many Northern churches, and groups of abolitionists prayed for his soul. John's death showed that some White people were willing to put their lives on the line for their Black brothers and sisters. Others were spurred to join his campaign, and this became one of the main causes of the American Civil War of 1861–1865. The resulting defeat of the slave-owning Southern states led to the final abolition of slavery throughout North America. John never saw it – but his dream had come true.

'Though a White gentleman, [Brown] is in sympathy a Black man, and as deeply interested in our cause, as though his own soul had been pierced with the iron of slavery.'
(Frederick Douglass, African-American anti-slavery campaigner)

During the Civil War, many soldiers of the Union (Northern) army had a marching song. It is still sung today:

John Brown's body lies a-mouldering in the grave,
John Brown's body lies a-mouldering in the grave,
John Brown's body lies a-mouldering in the grave...
But his soul goes marching on.

What Do You Think?

1. Why do you think John Brown was so opposed to slavery? How was his position different from that of Sam Sharpe or Nat Turner?

2. John Brown gave up a peaceful life with his family in order to fight for something he believed in. Have you ever given up something for your beliefs (these do not have to be religious beliefs) or principles? What was it and how did it feel to do this?

3. What risks do you think were taken by the volunteers on the Underground Railroad? Why do you think they were prepared to help in this way?

4. John Brown's Christian faith motivated his anti-slavery work. Why do you think he turned from non-violent action to violence? How might he have squared the violence with his Christian faith?

Fighting for Freedom

How do you resist evil without becoming evil yourself? Sam Sharpe, Nat Turner, and John Brown all resisted the brutal injustice of human slavery in the early 19th century – and all three paid the price for it by hanging. They devoutly believed that God was with them in their struggles, although Sam is possibly the only one remembered now with much affection. He was completely against the use of violence, following the words of Jesus:

'Those who draw the sword shall die by the sword.'
(MATTHEW 26:52)

Four non-violent protesters

Desmond Tutu

Gandhi

Martin Luther King

Aung San Suu Kyi

One thing is very clear from these stories – that making an act of violence, even for the best of reasons, can have consequences far beyond our control *and sometimes even makes the situation worse*. Sam's alternative path of determined peaceful resistance still posed a serious threat to the slave-owners – and his tactics were mirrored in the successful protests of other world leaders who later advocated non-violence, such as Mahatma Gandhi and Martin Luther King. *Imagine* what might have happened after 1831 if some of his followers *hadn't* turned to violence – what might the consequences have been for slaves and slave-owners in Jamaica, the Caribbean – and, who knows, even America?

What Do You Think?

1. Sam Sharpe, Nat Turner and John Brown were all very different. They each died for what they believed in. Each could be described as a 'freedom fighter'. Which, if any, of them do you admire and why?

2. Does the end ever justify the means? Give reasons for your answer.

Biographical Notes

1800	Nat Turner born Virginia, America
1800	John Brown born Connecticut, America
1801	Sam Sharpe born Montego Bay, Jamaica
1803	William Knibb born Kettering, UK
1807	British Parliament passes Act to Abolish the Slave Trade
1823	Amelioration Bill passed by British Parliament
1831	Nat Turner leads rebellion
1831	Nat Turner executed
1831	Christmas Rebellion, Jamaica
1832	Sam Sharpe hanged
1833	British Parliament passes Slave Emancipation Act
1833	William Knibb recalled to Britain
1834	William Knibb returns to Jamaica
1838	Slavery finally abolished in Britain and all its colonies
1849	Harriet Tubman escapes northwards on the 'Underground Railway'
1855	John Brown a conductor on the 'Underground Railway'
1855	John Brown sets up a safe haven for anti-slavery settlers
1856	John Brown attacks Pottawamonie Creek
1859	John Brown attacks Harpers Ferry
1859	John Brown hanged
1865	Slavery finally abolished in the United States
1925	Epic poem 'John Brown's Body' written by Stephen Vincent Benét
1943	Benét awarded Pulitzer Prize for 'John Brown's Body'

Things to Do

1 For each of Sam Sharpe, Nat Turner and John Brown, write three diary entries that they might have written: (a) on the day before their final act that led to their arrest, (b) on the day after it had gone wrong, and (c) on the day they awaited execution. Include reflections on what they believed, their motives, their hopes and their fears.

2 Imagine that in 2007, the bicentenary of the Act to Abolish the Slave Trade, you are asked to devise a memorial in England to either Sam Sharpe, Nat Turner or John Brown, who were all executed for their efforts to abolish slavery. Who would you choose? Why? What would be an appropriate memorial and where would you place it? Design your chosen memorial and annotate the design to explain the significance of each part of it. If practical, make a model.

3 What are the similarities and differences between Nat Turner, Sam Sharpe and John Brown? Think about their lives, what they did, what they believed, how other people viewed them and their influence on the campaign against slavery. You could use a Venn diagram to show what the three men have in common and the differences between them.

4 What positive and negative effects did the Christmas Rebellion of 1831 have? Was Sam Sharpe a hero or a villain? In pairs, script and/or record two imaginary conversations between people with different views on these questions: (a) two slaves and (b) two modern human rights activists. Each person should give reasons for their opinions. You could choose a real person such as Martin Luther King as one of the modern activists.

5 EITHER
Find out about one or more campaigners who have used non-violent means of protest, e.g., Gandhi, Martin Luther King, Aung San Suu Kyi.

(a) What are the similarities and differences between their approaches and that planned by Sam Sharpe?

(b) What qualities does a good leader need to have? Which leadership qualities did Sam Sharpe have and how did he use them? Compare Sam as a leader with the non-violent campaigners you have researched.

OR
Imagine that, whilst in prison awaiting his trial, Sam had the opportunity to write a letter to campaigners coming after him. What advice might Sam have given them about leadership, non-violent protest and what he had learned from his experiences? Draft Sam's letter.

6 The abolition campaign in England in the 1830s included boycotts of food produced in the slave plantations of the West Indies and America. Find out about modern campaigns that have encouraged consumer boycotts. What were these campaigns targeting? How successful were they?

7 Organise a class debate on 'We believe that non-violent protest was more effective than the use of violence in bringing about the abolition of slavery'.

8 (a) Is it possible or desirable to forgive people who have treated you very badly? Visit www.forgiveness.org and read a selection of stories about forgiveness. Do you think the people in those stories were right to forgive? Give reasons. Try to find out what the family of Anthony Walker (murdered in Liverpool in 2005) said about forgiving his killers.

(b) Find out about the Truth and Reconciliation Commission established by Archbishop Desmond Tutu in South Africa after Apartheid ended. In what ways could a similar initiative be applied to the legacy of Transatlantic Slavery?

(c) Use your research to prepare a school assembly about slavery, addressing issues of forgiveness, truth and reconciliation.

9 Why were missionaries in Jamaica in the 1820s reluctant to challenge slavery? What instructions did the missionary societies give them? Do you think religion and politics should be kept separate? Why?/Why not? Choose three volunteers to 'hot seat' as William Knibb: (a) in the Thomas Burchell Baptist Church in Jamaica in 1830, (b) on 23 May 1832, when Sam Sharpe was executed, (c) after his speech in Exeter Hall, England in August 1832. Find out what he believes about slavery, how he feels about the situation of the slaves, what (if anything) he has done or plans to do and why.

10 Nat Turner believed that God guided him by supernatural signs. Give two or more examples of stories in the Bible where God uses such signs to warn or guide people. Invite a Christian visitor into the class to answer questions about how they believe that God communicates with them today and how they interpret supernatural signs. (Christian representatives from different churches may have different views about this.) Before the visit, draft a set of questions to ask.

11 Find different accounts of Nat Turner's story. (You could use an Internet search.) Can you find any reports written at the time? Is he portrayed as a hero or villain, victor or victim?

12 (a) Read the Bible passages Matthew 22:34-40, Genesis 1:26-27, Romans 10:12, Colossians 3:11, Galatians 3:28. Also read Ephesians 6:5-9, but remember that in New Testament times slaves were common and many were servants who were well educated, and had very responsible jobs in households.

(b) Imagine you are Sam Sharpe. Draft a speech to use at church explaining why, as a Christian, you believe slavery to be wrong and what the Bible says that supports your belief. Role play Sam Sharpe preaching, with other slaves asking him questions.

Religious and Moral Education Press
A division of SCM-Canterbury Press Ltd
A wholly owned subsidiary of
Hymns Ancient & Modern Ltd
St Mary's Works, St Mary's Plain,
Norwich, Norfolk NR3 3BH

Story copyright © 2007 Uzoamaka Agyare-Kumi

Questions copyright © 2007 The Stapleford Centre

Uzoamaka Agyare-Kumi has asserted her right under the Copyright, Designs and Patents Act, 1988, to be identified as Author of this Work.

All rights reserved. No part of this publication may be reproduced, stored in a retrieval system, or transmitted, in any form or by any means, electronic, electrostatic, magnetic tape, mechanical, photocopying, recording or otherwise, without permission in writing from the publishers.

First published 2007

ISBN 978 1 85175 342 0

Designed and typeset by
TOPICS – The Creative Partnership, Exeter

Printed in Great Britain by Brightsea Press, Exeter for SCM-Canterbury Press Ltd, Norwich

Notes for Teachers

The first *Faith in Action* books were published in the late 1970s and the series has remained popular with both teachers and pupils. However, much in education has changed over the last twenty years, such as the development of both new examination syllabuses in Religious Studies and local agreed syllabuses for Religious Education which place more emphasis on pupils' own understanding, interpretation and evaluation of religious belief and practice, rather than a simple knowledge of events. This has encouraged us to amend the style of the *Faith in Action* Series to make it more suitable for today's classroom.

The aim is, as before, to tell the stories of people who have lived and acted according to their faith, but we have included alongside the main story questions which will encourage pupils to think about the reasons for the behaviour of our main characters and to empathise with the situations in which they found themselves. We hope that pupils will also be able to relate some of the issues in the stories to other issues in modern society, either in their own area or on a global scale.

The 'What Do You Think?' questions may be used for group or class discussion or for short written exercises. The 'Things to Do' at the end of the story include ideas for longer activities for RE or Citizenship and offer opportunities for assessment.

In line with current syllabus requirements, as Britain is a multifaith society, Faith in Action characters are selected from a variety of faith backgrounds and many of the questions may be answered from the perspective of more than one faith.

Acknowledgements

This is one of three *Faith in Action* books and a Teacher's Resource on CD-ROM published in association with **set all free** ACT TO END SLAVERY, a project of Churches Together in England to commemorate the bicentenary in 2007 of the Act to Abolish the Slave Trade. Further information can be found at www.setallfree.net

These publications have been developed by the **set all free** education group, consisting of Uzoamaka Agyare-Kumi, Linda Ali, Alison Farnell, Sarah Lane, Tessa Oram, Richard Reddie, Sally Smith and Kate Yates, who have all made significant contributions to the content.

Staff at The Stapleford Centre have helped to produce this series – www.stapleford-centre.org
Anti-Slavery International has given invaluable help in providing images to be used in this publication – www.antislavery.org